Sandy

The Autobiography of a Star

as told to **William Berloni**
and **Allison Thomas**

SCHOLASTIC BOOK SERVICES
New York Toronto London Auckland Sydney Tokyo

PHOTO CREDITS

The authors wish to thank the following for permission to reproduce the
photographs that appear in the book: Michael Carr, pages 23, 24, 26, 36,
38, 39, 44, 47, 52, 53, 55, 70, 77, 82, 83, 85, 88, 90, 91, 93, 94; Wolfgang
Kurth, page 87; *New York Post,* page 81 (Vernon Shibla), page 84 (Joe
DeMaria); Martha Swope, frontispiece, pages 78, 79; The White House
(official photograph), page 74; Bill Yoscary, pages 48, 49.

ISBN 0-590-31303-7

12 11 10 9 8 7 6 5 4 3 2 1   10   2 3 4 5 6/8

Printed in the U.S.A.   11

This book is gratefully dedicated by Sandy to
ELEANOR and **PHIL BERLONI**
with love

Acknowledgments

So many people have helped us all along our career that it's hard to name them all, but Billy and I wish to specially thank and acknowledge the following people. Alphabetically, they are *Annie* and her creators, casts, crews, and coordinators; Michael Carr; Martin Charnin; the Connecticut Humane Society; the Dawn Animal Agency; Jude De Prospo; the Friends of George Spelvin; John Hoyt, President, Humane Society of the United States; Andrea McArdle; Kristene Mothersele, New York University Drama Department; David Powers; Michael Price; Mr. and Mrs. Roger Stevens; Martha Swope; Norma Terris; Earl Wilson; the Yonkers Animal Shelter; and Bill Yoscary.

One

I was born in a barn, sometime late in 1974. Although mutts like me don't usually have birthdays, I have two. I celebrate one in November and one in May. But that's all part of the story.

Up in northwestern Connecticut, where the New York and Massachusetts borders meet, was where I first saw the light of day. My mother was the farm airedale and she worked hard, guarding the chickens from the foxes and weasels who would have killed them if they could. Dad was a big, handsome dog, although I never knew him, and I'm sure that he was at least part Irish wolfhound, because I've inherited his face and, Mama told me, his large, melting brown eyes. I had two sisters and a brother, and we were a happy, healthy bunch of lively pups.

But the farm needed only one working dog, and my mother was it. One by one, my sisters and brother said goodbye and went off to new homes, until only Mama and I were left.

Since I was a yard dog, not a house dog, I didn't come in for much petting or human affection, outside of an occasional pat or "good boy" when I'd done a job well. But I didn't miss it. I had Mama and I had all the busy excitement of the farm. I used to bark at the chickens to watch them scatter, but Mama, who took her work very seriously, would nip my ears when I did that. There was a cat there, but he was almost as big as I was and I didn't dare chase him. In fact, he chased me, and he always looked like he meant business, so I stayed clear of his claws. I liked the horses, because they were so tall and handsome, but best of all I liked the patient, fragrant cows.

Winter came late that year, and while Mama was busy working I'd rush through the dry leaves that had piled up around the farm, because I loved the rustling sound they made under my paws. When the cold weather came, bringing snow, I slept by Mama's side in the cozy barn with my friends the cows, surrounded by the sweet smell of hay and the cows' warm breath.

But winter passed finally, and I came into my first spring bigger and more rambunctious, ready for play. So, when a family of cousins visited the farm for a week, I fell for their little boy, David, and he fell for me. It was the first time I had a playmate of my own age, and we would chase each other around the yard until we were both breathless. I would bark and he would shout, and my tail never stopped wagging.

When the time came for David's family to leave, I heard him begging his mother and father to take me with them, and at last they agreed. I was going to have my own home! Sorry as I was to leave Mama and the cows, I had a great curiosity about the world outside, and I had come to love David very much. He was the first human to give me affection, head-rubs and strokings, and I used to lick his face while he giggled with the tickling.

And soon I even got my name. Sandy. We drove from the farm for several hours until we reached the beaches of Long Island

Sound. David's family lived near Bridgeport, but they had rented a summer place on the beach. David had been calling me "Doggie," but when he first saw the beach he said, "Look! The sand is exactly the same color as his fur. I'm going to name him Sandy."

That summer was wonderful! The days were long and filled with sunshine and play. David and I spent most of the time at the beach, chasing after a yellow beach ball, checking out what floated in on the tide, running after each other and knocking each other over in the soft sand. Mostly I knocked David over—we weighed about the same, fifty pounds.

By now I had grown to full size, even though I was still a puppy at heart. I stayed real skinny, not that I was a picky eater. I ate whatever was being handed out—dog food, table scraps, even lobster one night when we had a clambake on the beach. I'm still skinny today. Sometimes I missed Mama, but I knew she was having a happy life. And so was I, with somebody to love who loved me back.

I had a real scare once. There was a strong current in the water near some rocks, and David had been warned about it, but one day he did go in there. I saw him slip down and go under, and there was suddenly a lot of splashing and no David. Even though I couldn't swim, I dashed into the water, dived down for him, grabbed him by the seat of his bathing suit, and tugged with all my strength. Both of us came up with our noses full of water, and we kept coughing it up for an hour. We were safe and sound, all except David's bathing suit, which my teeth had ripped. David's mom and dad were angry about the bathing suit, and David was afraid to tell them he'd disobeyed, so I was the one who was punished—no supper that night, and I had to sleep under the porch instead of in the house.

After all the lights were out and the family was asleep, David snuck out of the house and whispered to me, and I crawled out from under the porch. He brought me a peanut butter and jelly sandwich to show me he was sorry. Peanut butter and jelly is not my favorite dish, but I ate it all up to show my boy that I loved him, and I *was* hungry.

And then summer came to an end, and with it so did my happiness. In the last week of the vacation, I could hear David's dad and mom talking a lot about me. They kept looking at me and mentioning my name, but never when David was around. They said I was too big, too clumsy, that I ate too much, that I'd be in the way. But they didn't seem happy; their faces were always worried, and they kept their voices low, as if they didn't want to be overheard.

And then, one terrible day, I saw David being half dragged, half carried to the car, yelling, "Sandy! Sandy!" as if his heart would break. What was happening? Why was he crying? Was he hurt? His mother pulled him into the back seat with her, and his father started up the motor. I ran toward the car; were they forgetting to take me? The car began to move and I ran after it, barking as loudly as I could. I was scared and bewildered because I could hear David crying from the back seat and calling my name. As the car went faster and faster, I ran faster, but there was no way that I could keep up with it.

I chased that car up the road for as long as it was in sight, but in a few minutes it had disappeared. My paws sore and burning, I limped back to the house and crawled under the porch. I couldn't understand what had happened. Where had they gone? Why was David crying? Why had they left me behind?

I expected them to come back any minute; my ears kept pricking for the sound of an automobile. But the road was empty. I stayed by the house for several days, waiting for David to come running up with our yellow beach ball for me to chase. But David never came. I became hungrier and hungrier, but there was nothing to eat. The house was locked; my bowl was empty. My stomach kept growling for food, and, suddenly, I knew that I was *alone!*

If David's parents knew I had once saved his life, would it have made a difference? They knew how much we loved each other, but they had no room in their life for a dog, not even me. Hope began to fade that I'd ever see David again, and I knew that if I stayed by the house any longer I'd starve; I had to go in search of food.

The beach in autumn is a bare and deserted place. I sniffed around the tidal wrack, but I don't eat seaweed, and I couldn't even eat the mussels that clung to the clumps of weed. Something

moved across the sand and I chased it, but this turned out to be a mistake. The something turned out to be a crab that scuttled into a hole in the sand, leaving me with a bleeding paw. I couldn't catch birds or fish. My mother hadn't raised me to be a hunter. And the hungrier I got, the weaker I became. I had to go find food before it was too late.

The only other place I knew of as home was the farm, but that was so far away. Still, it was the only place to go, and I had to try to find it. I knew that it was in the direction away from the beach, so I tried to forget my memories of David and our games, of the fun and the affection we'd shared, and I started on the long journey north. I yearned for sweet water to drink, a warm place in the barn, and food to fill my emptiness.

The next weeks are a blur to me, a painful blur of unkind words and stones chucked at a skinny stray dog. I got an occasional handout, and I wolfed down anything offered to me: bread, cheese, scraps of meat, once—oh, joy!—spaghetti and a meatball. But what I needed most was shelter, a home, and love. And nobody offered me that.

Not that I could blame them much. I was a mess. My ribs stuck out and my coat got all matted and I was a wretched sight. I kept going, though, my nose pointed north. Whenever I came to a town, I would look for a butcher shop. If I was lucky enough to find one, I'd sit in front of the window and stare in, my hungry heart in my hungry eyes. I must have been pitiful, because every butcher I ever came across gave me something to eat. Mostly gristle and fat, but delicious just the same, and it kept me going. But I couldn't always find a butcher. Most people shop in supermarkets nowadays, and all the signs say "No dogs allowed," so somebody always chased me out before I could locate the meat section.

Early in my travels, I learned to avoid the highways whenever I could. The cars and trucks went by so fast, bearing down from both directions at once, scaring me so I couldn't move. And I once

saw the smashed body of a dog at the side of the road. I will never be able to shake that memory; it is burned into my brain. When I saw that dog, I knew that if I wasn't *very* careful, I could end up the same way.

So I mainly traveled by the back roads, through small towns and past farmhouses. All that kept me going was the memories of my mother and my David—surely there must be a home for me somewhere! Somewhere there must be somebody to love me and take me in, accepting my love in return. I remember the first big farm I saw on my travels. It looked and smelled so homey and familiar that a great longing welled up inside me. Could there be a place for me there?

But dogs were already living there, and they didn't want a mangy stranger like me. When first they came running, I thought they wanted to make friends, but instead they attacked me, three of them. It was one of the most terrifying moments of my life. They were snapping and snarling around me, and I turned tail and ran for my life, but hunger and traveling had left me tired and weak, and they caught up with me. They knocked me to the ground, and I was certain my last hour had come.

If the dinner bell hadn't rung that very minute, I might not be telling this story. But as soon as the three of them heard "Food!" they ran off and left me alone to lick my wounds. But I didn't stop to lick; instead I ran until I dropped down exhausted. I had received a couple of slashes that would take weeks to heal. I was so miserable that I lay down to die. There wasn't an inch of me that wasn't hurting, and hunger had made me so dizzy I could hardly see or hear. All my cuts and bruises were aching, but I can't tell you what was hurting the most—the pain, the hunger or the loneliness. I laid my weary chin on my aching paws, and shut my eyes, not knowing if I would ever open them again.

And then—a man's kind voice! A man was patting me and telling me it would be all right, a man was picking me up and carrying me into a warm house. I saw bright lights, and they hurt my eyes, but kind hands were washing my cuts, and kind hands were putting dog food into a bowl and I fell asleep filled with food and the memory of kind hands.

When I woke up, I found myself in a cage. I didn't know where I was at first, only that I was surrounded by metal bars. Around me were other cages, and cats and dogs were in them. I could hear barking and yelping and mewing. And there was a strange smell, too, a sharp odor I couldn't place. But it was a clean smell.

I was in luck. Of all places to collapse, I had accidentally found the driveway of an animal hospital. The doctor had found me and brought me inside. It was he who had patched me up and fed me.

But, once more, I didn't seem to fit in anywhere. The hospital was a small one; cages were needed for other animals, and the doctor had two dogs of his own already. He just didn't know what to do with me. "I wish I could keep you, boy," he told me. "You're a good fella, but I just have no place to put you. You can stay with me until you're feeling better, then we'll see if I can find you a home somewhere."

I stayed in that animal hospital for about a week, mostly eating and sleeping to get my strength back. Twice a day I ran with the other dogs in large outdoor runs, for exercise. I ate all the time, endlessly, hungrily emptying my bowl as soon as it was filled. The doctor himself was surprised at how much I was eating and how little I showed it. And I lapped up a lot of cool, sweet water, remembering the muddy stuff I had had to drink out of standing pools and puddles. Nothing will ever taste as good as that fresh water, and I licked my dish dry twice a day.

But soon the doctor was needing the cage for another dog, and he kept trying, without success, to find me a home. It seems that everybody loves a puppy, but nobody wants to adopt a full-grown dog. Every day, a happy owner came to the hospital to reclaim a beloved pet, but nobody ever came for me.

Then, one day, the doctor brought a young woman to see me. She smoked a lot of cigarettes, and had a nervous, anxious face. But she looked me over and told the doctor I'd do, and came the next day to pick me up in a van. We drove to a flower store. It was her store, and it was filled with the most wonderful colors and smells; the flowers reminded me of the country. She was to be my new owner, and I wagged my tail hopefully at her and jumped around her happily, but she wouldn't let me kiss her face. She gave me one or two halfhearted pats.

I was sorry to leave the doctor, because he'd been so kind to me, but I was so anxious for a home of my own that I went along without question. I think of him a lot, even today, and always with gratitude, because he saved my life.

I thought a new life was beginning for me now; I had a new owner, a new home, a *place* for me. I thought I'd be surrounded by love and by the sweet scents of the flowers in the store. But the woman who took me didn't care for dogs and didn't want me for a pet. She wanted a ratter! There were rats in her basement, and they terrified her. Frankly, they terrified me, too. My mother would have known how to handle them, because she was all terrier. But I'm only part terrier, and the other part of me didn't want to leave the warm, fragrant upstairs and go down into a cold, dank, smelly cellar and see beady red eyes glowing in the dark. No sir! As for actually doing battle with a rat, forget it! I have always been peace-loving, and I always will be, especially where one of those scary animals is concerned. It took only two evenings for the combination of the dark and the scuttling sounds to get to me and send me out onto the road again, looking for Mama and the farm.

Two

*I*t was pretty cold the night I sneaked out of the cellar and headed north. Autumn was nearly over, and winter drawing in. The days were short and the nights long and getting more and more bitter. I was hungry again, all the time, and I couldn't find my way out of town. Garbage cans, especially the ones outside restaurants or butcher shops, became my only sources of food. Often I was chased away from them by other starving dogs, even by cats. One night, on the outskirts of the city, I had a run-in with a raccoon over a good can of scraps, and I'm ashamed to say the raccoon won.

And then I woke up one morning to white all around me— even in my ears and nose. I got very scared that I would never see my home again. I was lost, everything was white with snow, and I was cold and hungry. I shivered all the time, and the world was so covered in snow that I left my pawprints everywhere, and I noticed that they sometimes went around in circles—I was covering ground that I had covered before. Again, nobody wanted to give me a home. Nobody had that special face with the special smile of welcome, nobody wanted to keep me warm. I had no name now; it went with having no home. Soon I began to doubt that I'd ever had a home. Maybe I'd only dreamed it. Maybe I only dreamed about David and the beach, and the kind doctor. If I could fall asleep at all, I twitched and shivered in my dreams, reminded only of fear and hunger.

I learned to sleep curled up at the roots of large old trees. They gave me protection from the wind, and the ground was softer and less icy there. Occasionally, I'd come across a barn where there was no rival dog, and I'd sleep warm and happy with the sweet-smelling, patient cows. Many nights I slept under the porches of people's houses, or in the sheltered alleyways of the cities. When it rained, I slept under a truck, hearing the heavy patter of the drops on the metal roof above me. I learned simple survival tricks—how to scrounge a meal out of nowhere, how to find the least shivery corner, how to avoid other dogs and stray cats, and how to avoid those people who threw stones or aimed kicks at me. I just kept going.

One night I found myself back at the highway. The night was very dark; there wasn't any moon. The road itself was a black ribbon, down which lights would rush with no warning, bringing noise and sudden danger. But my path north led over the other side of that four-lane highway. I had to chance it.

Slowly at first, then with more speed, I began to trot across the road. Suddenly, as though it had been waiting for me, a huge monster with glaring eyes came roaring out of the dark. I stopped moving, frozen by the gleam of the headlights. I wanted to flee, but in what direction? Forward? Back to the roadside? The eyes came closer and closer, and I had a sudden vision of that other dog's crushed body. The noise of the truck deafened my ears. I began to tremble and whimper, paralyzed by fear.

With a shriek of brakes, the truck pulled to a halt only a couple of yards from where I stood, frozen in my tracks. I could hear a door open, and a man's deep voice talking to himself. "It's a dog! I nearly killed some mutt!"

I heard the clumping of boots, then a tall figure knelt beside me. "Are you all right, boy? I didn't hit ya. No, not a scratch on ya, just scared half to death. What are ya doin' on the road this time of night, anyway? I might have smashed ya flat."

He had a rough kindness in his voice that made me thump my tail on the ground weakly. I liked him right away, and hoped he'd like me.

"Go on, boy. Scoot. I can't take you."

I walked away slowly, but only a few feet, then I sat down on the road in the glare of the headlights, and looked at the big man, my heart in my eyes.

"Go on, now. Go along. I got to be moving, and I ain't got time to fool with you."

I sat without moving, except for the thump of my tail. I wanted this human to want me, to save me and take care of me.

"Okay, fella, I'll give you a lift. I guess I can't leave you here. But once we get to Hartford, out ya go. I ain't got room in my life for no dog."

He lifted me into the truck and we drove for over an hour, me spread out exhausted on the front seat next to him. Once we stopped at a twenty-four-hour diner, and he brought me out a warm hamburger wrapped in greasy paper. I polished it off in nothing flat, then I touched my paw to his thigh to say thank you. When he rubbed my ears, I thought I was in heaven.

By the time we got to Hartford, we were friends. I kissed his face and thumped my tail, and he patted me just right. His name was Harry, and he called me Charley. He drove a big semi on long

19

hauls and he decided to take me with him for company. I'd sit up beside him and wag my tail just from the pleasure of being with Harry. The days grew warm, and I lived happily on roadside hamburgers and containers of milk and frequent pats on the head. Harry wasn't married, and whenever we got home to Hartford we'd spend a lot of time in front of the television set, Harry watching the shows, and me napping on the rug near his chair. It was a quiet life, and a good one.

But it didn't last very long. One night, Harry got sick. He fell down and turned real white, and people came to take him away. In all the excitement, the neighbors forgot me, and I was locked out and left behind. All I could do was sit outside and bark, and I barked miserably until somebody threw something at me to chase me away. I couldn't find Harry, and nobody would come to the door and let me in. I stayed in front of our house and barked until morning.

Nobody around there wanted me, and the kids and grownups tried to get rid of me by yelling and throwing things, and even once taking a stick to me. But I wouldn't leave, just in case Harry came back. So I'd bark all night long, and the neighbors would get more and more angry, because I didn't let them sleep.

After several days of this, I was a mess. I was hungry, thirsty, exhausted, and nearly crazy. I jumped and growled whenever anybody in the neighborhood came near me, and I was getting a bad name. People thought I might bite their children. I would never bite a child, but I can see why they were afraid. I was half starved, and very nervous; I barked all the time; everything and everybody spooked me. And Harry wasn't coming back.

One morning early, as I was lying near the house in a twitching sleep, strong hands grabbed me and tied a rope to my collar. I was dragged to a car and driven to a large building. The pound. Without a word or a goodbye, I was left there. I could hear frantic barking all around me, and I crouched with my tail between my legs, out of my senses with fear. A dog pound is the end of the line. I had heard that these places could keep you only a short time, then they had to put you to sleep.

My new and temporary home was to be a cage. It was a fairly large cage, and there was water and food in it, but it was still a cage. And I wasn't alone in it. There were two German shepherds with loud barks sharing it with me. *Grrrrrr. Wooof. Grrrrrrr! Rowf!* Maybe they were trying to make friends with me; I was afraid to find out. Seeking the darkest corner of the cage, I scrunched down and made myself as small as possible. I felt that I would never leave this cage until I was put to sleep. The people were kind, but they were fighting a losing battle. They couldn't keep us all. The lucky ones were adopted, but the lucky ones were few and far between. I knew I was never going to be one of the lucky ones.

I spent days in the corner of that cage, barely eating or drinking. I wouldn't go near the shelter people, even when they spoke to me gently. I was really confused by humans and didn't want anyone to ever touch me again.

Then, one day, it rained hard. We dogs ran in the outside runs rain or shine, for exercise. By the time I got back into the cage, my coat was soaked through. I must have looked a sight. I was thin, wet, sad-faced—the largest drowned rat in the world. But I didn't care. All I wanted was to be left alone, to sleep. When the door opened and somebody came in, the dogs all set up their usual "look at me" racket. Any time anybody walked into the pound, they all barked at the top of their lungs, hoping to be noticed. Hoping to be

adopted. I just kept to my corner, silent, making myself as invisible as possible.

A skinny young man came down the aisle of cages, and the two German shepherds ran forward, scratching at the bars, jumping up, barking and yelping. The young man looked at all the dogs, one by one, talking to someone from the shelter. They came to my cage, and I saw him peer in at me. He had a nice face, gentle, with large brown eyes just like mine.

"No, he's not the dog you want. I couldn't recommend this dog for your purposes. He's been beaten, and he just doesn't take to people anymore," I heard the shelter man say. Was he talking about me?

But the young man wasn't listening. He was kneeling by the side of the cage, as close as he could get to my corner, and he was holding out a dog biscuit to me, calling me over in the softest, sweetest voice I have ever heard.

"Here, boy, come here. Your ears are all wrong, and they probably won't want you, but I think you're beautiful. Come here, boy."

Something stirred inside me, and I was surprised to find myself on my feet, walking over to the boy, sticking my long nose out of the bars, eating the dog biscuit, letting him stroke and fondle my head and ears. His hand smelled like a good person's hand.

"I have to take a picture of him," the young man said. "I have to get him approved before I can adopt him."

But the attendant was shaking his head. "No way. His time is up, and he's going to be put to sleep tomorrow, first thing."

"Put to sleep? You *can't!* Look, I really want this dog. But I have to have an okay. The decision isn't mine. Please. I'll come back. I really will."

I could hear the worry and the sincerity in the boy's voice. But

the shelter man couldn't change his decision. "If you want him, you have to take him now. Because tomorrow he's not going to be here."

They opened the cage door, and I came out slowly. The boy knelt again and stroked my wet, wiry fur. I trembled, but I didn't move away as his hand passed over my back and flanks, feeling each individual rib; there was almost nothing under my coat except bones. Then he snapped my picture with a small camera.

"How much?" he asked the shelter man.

"Eight dollars." Meaning me. I cost eight dollars.

"I haven't got it with me," said the brown-eyed young man. "I've got only two dollars. Can I leave two dollars as a deposit and bring the rest tomorrow?"

Please, I begged silently. Please say yes.

"No." The attendant shook his head. "I'm sorry, but we cannot take deposits. You understand, don't you?"

I understood. I understood that tomorrow morning would be too late; there'd be no more me. The boy turned to go, and he and the man from the shelter moved away up the aisle of cages, still talking.

Don't go! Take me with you! Why did you pet me and feed me if you were going to leave me here to die? I saw them reach the door, and a deep sense of loss stole over me. I moved back into the shadows of the cage.

At the door, the boy turned and looked at me again. "I'll come back for you. I promise, Sandy. You'll see. You're going to be Sandy."

"Sandy"! He called me Sandy! How did he know my name?

Three

*L*ater, I heard the story of my adoption so often that I learned it by heart. After *Annie* opened in Washington and became such a hit, and especially after the Broadway opening, my story—in a much shortened version—made a lot of newspapers, if not front pages. It began at the Goodspeed Opera House in East Haddam, Connecticut, that very summer.

Goodspeed is known as a summer repertory theater. It puts on three productions each season, and this year a new musical called *Annie* was the third show. Based on the comic strip "Little Orphan Annie," the show needed a dog to play Sandy, Annie's dog. Bill Berloni, who worked as a carpenter in the set-building shop and doubled as an actor, was picked to select and train the dog, because he'd owned dogs all his life. Only nineteen, Bill was the skinny boy who'd come to the Newington shelter, the Connecticut Humane Society, and found me.

I was all wrong for the part. It wasn't a big part, or a very important part, not then, anyway. The only thing everybody agreed on was that Sandy should be medium size, of no particular breed, and have a sandy-colored coat and stick-up ears, like the comic strip. I am medium size, my breed is unrecognizable, and you know I have a sandy-colored coat. But my ears flop over. They definitely do not stick up, they flop. The ears were all-important, and mine were all wrong.

But Billy said many times that it was my eyes, my large, dark, melting eyes, that made up his mind. When he left the shelter with a snapshot of me, his mind was in turmoil, just like mine, and his heart was as heavy as mine. He wanted me, he felt sorry for me, but he believed that nobody at Goodspeed would approve of me for the part. The producer and director of *Annie* were away in New York, and I was slated to be put to sleep first thing the next morning.

All that night, Billy lay awake, trying to decide. He had shown my photograph to the technical crew, his friends at the shop, and they'd all told him no.

"The ears are all wrong," they told him. "He's too skinny. He'll never do. He doesn't look like the comic strip. You're crazy to even think about him."

But Billy did think about me. He couldn't sleep; he couldn't even shut his eyes. He knew that if he adopted me and the producer and director didn't like me, he could never bring himself to take me back to the shelter. I'd be his forever. Billy already had a dog at home with his parents in Connecticut. In New York, where he lived when he wasn't at Goodspeed, his landlord didn't permit dogs. So what was he going to do with me if I didn't work out for the show?

But, as he told me later, my eyes kept coming back to haunt him. If they put me to death, he'd never be able to forgive himself.

So next morning at about six, with eight borrowed dollars, he drove back to the shelter and found me again. He waited outside until the doors opened so that he'd get to me before the attendants did, and he signed the papers to adopt me.

I was never so glad to see anybody in my whole life. I recognized him as soon as he came in the door, and my tail began to wag furiously. I hadn't wagged it in such a long time, because I had nothing to wag about. Now I did. I had a new owner—no, *more* than an owner, I had a new friend.

Billy had brought along two friends, Patrick and Jude. Pat drove, and Jude and Billy sat with me in the back of the pickup. Jude won my heart right away, because it was she who suggested stopping for hamburgers. My life had undergone the most glorious change. It was a beautiful summer day. There I sat, in the warm sunshine, riding in a truck with new friends and eating a Big Mac, on my way to the most wonderful life that any dog has ever lived.

I said before that I have two birthdays. One of them is May 19, because that's the day that Billy adopted me. The other is November 19. I must have been born right about that time of year, and that date is Bill Berloni's birthday. Now we share it.

Billy laughs now when he remembers how he introduced me to the Goodspeed technical crew, but at the time his heart was in his mouth. He led me into a large building filled with sets and tools.

"Here he is," he said.

The crew crowded around me, a group of strange, unknown faces. Everything was so strange; the faces and voices of the people, the size of the place, and even the smells were very different. Paint and raw wood, canvas and sawdust. Later I would come to love the smells, and the faces and voices, but now they terrified me. I shrank back against Billy's leg.

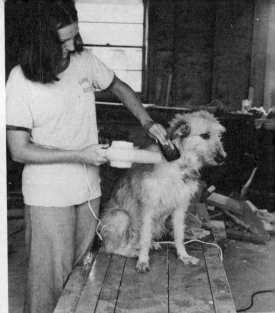
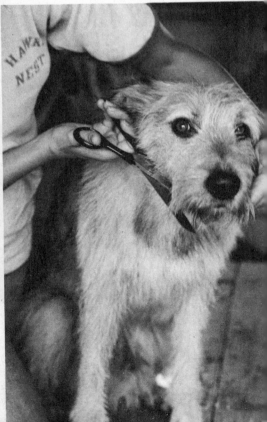

"He doesn't look anything like the comic strip," they said. Then they said, "Oh, the poor thing! He's so skinny and so frightened. Then they said, "He's soooo cute." Then they said, "He needs love, the darling." *Then* they said, "He needs a bath!"

A couple of the girls brought out a large iron tub and filled it up with water and soap and plunked me into it. Billy and my new friend Jude started scrubbing me down, holding me firmly and not letting me wiggle. I wasn't sure whether to bark or whine, whether to enjoy it or hate it, so I just sat there shivering, letting the soap and water happen. I knew Billy wouldn't hurt me.

They wrapped me in a big towel and rough-dried me, and that I liked. Then Jude began to blow my coat dry with a hair dryer, and *that* I *loved!* Nothing had ever felt as good as those warm gusts of air on my wet skin. I squirmed with happiness and pleasure, and rolled on my back, so that she could aim the dryer at my belly. I decided right there and then that if a bath led to this, I would have a bath every day of my life.

After I was dry, I looked a little better, but there were still matted places in my fur. Jude gave me a clipping, which sort of smoothed my coat down, but she got carried away when she went to trim my beard, getting it shorter on one side than the other. But I'm a nutty-looking dog anyway, and Billy decided that the lopsided look only added charm.

Now my life at Goodspeed was to begin. I had so much to learn. I had no idea what a theater was, or a stage. I had to get used to the place and the people. What was an audience? Why did they make that racket with their hands? Billy wanted me to start learning right away, even though he was still very uncertain if I'd really be Sandy. The producer and director were still in New York, and nobody had given me the go-ahead.

All the crew there began calling me Sandy right away. I was never anybody but Sandy to them. Billy took me everywhere with him, to the workshop, to the theater. I was shy and a little skittish at first, but I soon got used to the open sky and the green grass, and the smell of the Connecticut River, and I made myself familiar with all the trees. Little by little, I became adjusted to my freedom, to the regular meals, and to all the new people I was meeting. As long as Billy was with me, I was happy, and Billy was with me all the time. He even let me sleep on his bed, although his room was so small that the bed took up most of it, and I took up most of the bed.

Everything and everybody soon became familiar; the sights, sounds and smells began to sort themselves out, become a part of my life, the faces part of my family. There were about twenty people in the shop with Billy, and they all had a kind word and a pat for me. I began to feel secure.

When Billy worked in the shop, building scenery, he tied me up. But the rope was very long, and it never got in my way. It meant that I could stay outside or come indoors for shade, as I chose. When the sun got too hot, I'd nap in the shop, and when the bright day called to me I'd run around outside. I felt like a new dog.

In the evenings I'd go to the theater with Billy, because he had a part in the show that was running then. "Theater" was almost the first new word I learned at Goodspeed; Billy wanted me to get used to it right away. He was the only one who thought I had a chance at playing Sandy, even with my flop-over ears.

Most theaters have what they call a "greenroom," where the actors can sit and get ready to go on stage. Now that I have become an expert on greenrooms, I can tell you that Goodspeed's is pretty

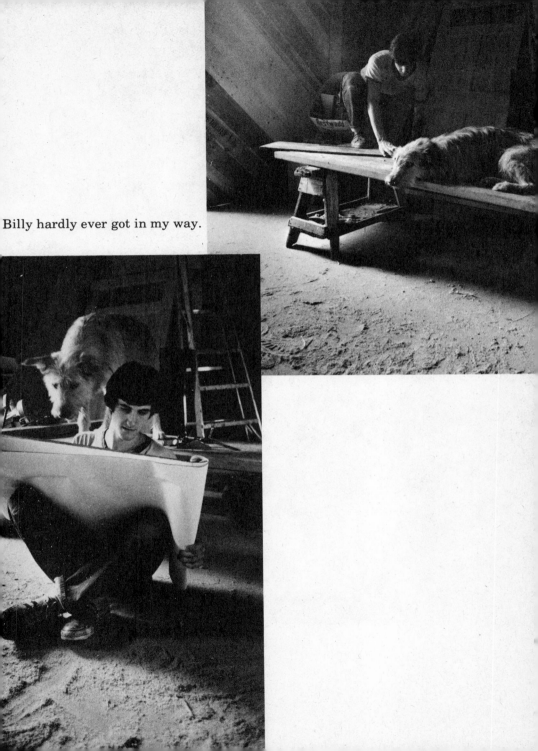

Billy hardly ever got in my way.

Burt Reynolds and I
may not always see eye to eye . . .
but I love opera,
and Beverly Sills loves me.

am just a little nosy about what Barbra Streisand
ay be wearing . . . and I am *never* afraid to take on
he Champ, Muhammad Ali.

modest, but it was my home when Billy was on stage. I'd wait for him there, all sprawled out on a black vinyl couch that became mine. The actors all made friends with me, and I enjoyed their company. At the end of the play, Billy would come and get me and take me to the wings, where I could see the audience sitting out there, and the footlights, and hear the clapping. Billy thought I should get used to all of that as quickly as possible.

The stage itself was different. If I was to be Sandy in the upcoming show, I'd have to learn a couple of simple tricks to do on stage every night. Billy decided to save the stage as a special place for us to play. He wanted us to play there every day, so that I would think of the stage as a happy place, our place, and know that I'd have a good time whenever I was on it. The only free time he had was his lunch hour, and every day, at noon, we'd go to the theater and play around on the stage, and eat our lunch there. Needless to say, I loved the stage from the very start.

Ever since I came to Goodspeed, I'd been hearing two names: Michael and Martin. Michael was Michael Price, executive producer of the Goodspeed Opera House, and Martin was Martin Charnin, the lyricist and director of *Annie,* Goodspeed's next production. It was up to Michael and Martin whether I was Sandy or whether Bill would have to find and train another dog. They were the two who were in New York at the time Billy adopted me.

One day, there was a lot of attention, and I was the center of it. I was brushed and combed, and my paw pads were cleaned, and my new collar was put on. Billy took me to the theater and sat me down on my favorite black vinyl couch. Then he said, "It's gonna happen. I know it. I feel it," and left me there.

Five minutes later he came back with another man. "Michael, I'd like you to meet Sandy."

Michael looked at me.

I looked at him.

"How much did he cost?" asked Michael.

"Eight dollars," said Billy, his voice quavering.

"Okay," said Michael. And he walked out of the greenroom.

With a big grin, Billy knelt beside the couch and put his arms around my neck. "That's it," he whispered. "You're Sandy. I knew it would happen. You're *in*."

I was on my way to becoming an actor.

But it wouldn't be easy, not for Billy and not for me, even though my part called for only a short series of tricks and I wouldn't be on stage for more than three minutes total. (Later, of course, when *Annie* became a smash hit, my part was greatly enlarged and became more complicated.) Bill Berloni was not a professional dog trainer, and I wasn't a professional dog. Almost any dog could have done as well as I. They had even been thinking of borrowing a local dog from its owner, but Billy had convinced them that it would be better to take a pound dog. It was his idea that, once that dog had been on the stage, it would be easy for him to find a home at the end of the summer.

If I had known then that Billy wasn't planning to keep me, I don't know what I'd have done. Maybe put my chin on my paws and closed my eyes forever. It's a good thing I didn't hear about that until long, long afterward.

I think I had better tell you a little something about *Annie* and my part in it, to give you an idea of what I had to learn. *Annie* is about a little orphan girl in New York in the 1930s. Because she's so cruelly treated in the orphanage, she runs away. While she's roaming the streets of Depression New York, she meets up with a stray mutt (played by me) who is running from the dog catchers. Because they are two of a kind, she befriends him, but a cop comes along and suspects he's a stray. Annie claims he's her dog, but the cop wants her to prove it. If he's your dog, what's his name? the policeman demands. Annie is stumped, but only for a second. I call him Sandy because of his sandy coat, she tells him. Oh yeah? If he's your dog Sandy, then call him. Let's see if he comes to you. So she calls, Sandy, Sandy . . . come here, Sandy. And you know that he *isn't* her dog, and you hold your breath to see if he'll come to her. And, suddenly, he does!

Then, more cops—this time to get Annie and take her back to the orphanage. Run, Sandy, run! she yells, and he runs off stage away from her, and they are parted for the rest of the play, only to be reunited in the very last scene, with a happy ending for both.

Well, that may not sound like much to you, but I had never learned a trick in my life, and Billy had never taught a trick in his life. And I had never acted on a stage. To me, the stage was the place for playing around.

The first thing I had to learn was to obey. How to sit on command, and lie down on command, how to heel, how to "speak." That wasn't hard to do, because Billy taught me in such a nice way. If somebody you love gives you a pat and a hug and a yummy for doing a simple little thing like sitting down, why, of course you'll do it. I did it to please Billy more than to get the yummy, although I *do* love snacks.

What I didn't know then was that Billy was teaching me some-

thing different. Dogs are usually taught by words, but he was teaching me to obey *hand* signals, not voice signals. Because, when I was on the stage, and he would be coaching me from the wings, he couldn't very well shout out commands for the whole audience to hear. So he'd point instead, or wave his hand, and I was supposed to obey.

So far, so good. I didn't know why he was doing what he was doing, but if he pointed his finger and I sat down, he'd give me a big hug and that was good enough for me.

Then he took me to the theater and started acting very crazy. He would get down on his belly and crawl across the stage. He was trying to show me something, but what? He'd crawl, and then he'd get up and look at me. And I'd look back at him.

"Crawl, Sandy," he'd plead.

What on earth for? I'd ask myself. I didn't realize that my part in the play called for me to crawl on stage for my first entrance.

"*Crawl,* Sandy." And down Bill would get and show me again. It didn't look at all enticing, comfortable or fun—it even brought back bad memories—and I wasn't at all interested in learning how to do it.

It became a favorite noontime treat for the staff to go down to the theater and watch Billy crawl. The technical crew would sit in the audience and laugh and clap their hands, and I enjoyed watching them watching us. I also loved to watch Billy get mad, because he'd jump up and down and turn red.

After a few days, Billy stopped crawling. Instead, he would lie down on top of me, pinning me to the stage. Then he'd move my front legs back and forth, and kind of drag me along the stage, yelling, "Crawl, Sandy, *crawl!*" Actually, that's not as uncomfortable as it sounds, because Billy doesn't weigh all that much. When he started to do this, our audience grew bigger and bigger, and

40

they laughed harder and clapped louder. I was enjoying all the attention, but I began to feel sorry for Billy. I knew he wanted me to do something for him that I wasn't doing. But Billy's technique worked—I learned the trick and crawled, finally. There was nothing I wouldn't do for Bill, once I understood.

I have never seen a human being so happy in his life as Bill Berloni was the day I crawled. If he'd had a tail, he would have wagged it. I thought he'd hug me to death.

"You can do anything!" he shouted. "You're the smartest dog in the world!"

I wriggled with pleasure and jumped up on him.

"Crawl, Sandy, *crawl!*"

Now I was getting used to the stage as a place to work, and I was so comfortable with it I'd often fall asleep in the middle of a command. Billy was moving farther and farther away from me, getting me accustomed to responding to his hands while he was in the wings and I was on the stage. Once I knew that it would take him a little while to cross the stage and yell at me, I'd sometimes give a large yawn and put my head on my paws for a little snooze. Never run when you can walk, never stand when you can sit, never sit when you can lie down, and take a nap when you lie down: that's my motto, and it used to make Billy mad.

After the crawl, all the other tricks came easy to both of us. Except one, which confused me. Billy would call me, and I would get up to answer him.

"Sandy. Sandy. No, no, go back. Don't get up."

Why couldn't he make up his mind? When you call me I come. No, he says, stay. Was I supposed to come or stay? Jump up or lie down? Answer or not answer? Meow like a cat? It was puzzling to me and it would have been puzzling to you too. It took me a while to get used to the fact that I wasn't supposed to come unless Billy called me and slapped his knee at the same time.

"Sandy. Sandy." Don't come.

"Sandy. Sandy." Slap. Come.

Once we went into rehearsals, it became very, very clear. Annie is trying to prove to the policeman that Sandy is her dog, when he isn't. I have to lie there and hear my name spoken, *and not respond to it*. Even when she calls me, I don't get up. That's what makes the audience hold its breath. Will he come or won't he?

"Sandy." Slap.

I get up and walk over to Annie and jump up on her with

affection—see, I really am her dog! The audience lets out its breath. That's theater. All done with a kneeslap invented by Billy.

Rehearsals. By now, the cast of *Annie* was arriving at Goodspeed. Most of them were little girls, who played the orphans, and one of them was Kristen Vigard, who played Annie. Rehearsals were about to begin.

Billy began by bringing my food to the theater and letting Kristen feed me.

"See, Sandy, here's who is feeding you. Kristen."

Now, I have yet to meet a child I don't like; I have loved them all. I have no idea why Billy ever thought I wouldn't do the same tricks for Kristen that I did for him. Why not? She was a terrific little girl, and we hit it off right away. As for the feeding, who did he think he was kidding? I knew who was carrying the food to the theater; I have eyes and a nose, don't I? And where food is concerned, I can see or smell through a brick wall. Kristen and I worked together with Billy one or two mornings a week, and she learned all the things I could do, and the cues that Billy had taught me for my tricks.

Then, just as everything was going well for all of us, and only a few weeks before *Annie* was to open, I nearly lost my life.

Four

It was brutally hot that day, and in the workshop everyone was cranky from heat and hard work. As usual, I was tied up outside, but I needed shade, because the heat was getting to me. I'd drunk a gallon of water that day, but my tongue was hanging out just the same. It was one of those days when no place you go is comfortable or cool. No wonder they call them the "dog days." Dogs really suffer in the heat.

The workshop was hot, but at least it was shady, and I kept going inside. It wasn't my fault that a freshly painted piece of scenery was directly underpaw. I don't like paint on my feet any more than they liked feet on their paint. But the screaming and yelling, just because I stepped on some scenery! Whew! I was banished, chucked out, evicted from the workshop. You'd think I had the mange, or rabies, the way they carried on.

Billy was upstairs and didn't see me, so somebody else untied me, marched me over the grass to a long distance away, and tied me up again. Now I couldn't reach the workshop.

But I couldn't reach shade either. There appeared to be nothing in sight, nothing except some old pickup trucks standing parked nearby. Still, they were better than nothing, because there were patches of shade underneath them, so I crept under the nearest one and did what any dog would do in such weather. I fell asleep.

The next thing I knew, I heard a sickening crunch, and a second later, the pain shooting through my body told me that the sickening crunch was me. What had happened? Where was Billy? I began to howl in pain, screaming for Billy. Why was I hurting like this?

I tried to stand up, but I was pinned down completely. My front legs could barely move, and my hind legs wouldn't obey me at all. Where was Billy? I was trapped here, helpless and in agony. Where was Billy?

As soon as the driver heard my cry, he stopped the pickup. How could he know I was there when he got in and put the truck in reverse? Only when he heard the crunch of my bones and my yelping did he get out and see my tail sticking out from under the back wheels. Instantly, he leaped back in the truck and drove forward, releasing me.

But I still couldn't move. My hind legs were useless, paralyzed. The pain was so strong I was crying, and I started to black out. Where was Billy?

"Don't touch him! Don't anybody move him!" It was Billy's voice, Billy's face, with tears streaming down the cheeks. Then he was gone, running like crazy.

He came back with a blanket, the keys to the van, and Patrick to drive it. All the way to the animal hospital he held my head cradled on his lap, crying and promising me that I was going to be all right. I don't think either one of us believed that, and I could barely hear him because I hurt so much.

The doctor wasn't sure I'd be okay, either. Only the X rays could tell, and he told Billy it would take overnight at least. Either my pelvis was broken or my back legs were dislocated. If my pelvis was broken, it might take between six and eight months to heal, and then I might never walk again. If it was a dislocation, it would be a far simpler matter.

The doctor gave me a shot, and the next hours were a blur of pain, of pain-killers, but mostly of fear. It wasn't until later the next day that I saw Billy again. The X rays had been taken and a diagnosis made. It was a dislocation, not a broken pelvis. The doctors would have to put me under anesthesia to reset my legs, and then I would go into a temporary cast. The vet said I was expected to walk again, and Billy said, "Thank God!"

Walk, yes. But now Billy was worried about whether I'd be able to appear on stage. It was only fourteen days to opening night. Could I crawl, and then walk over to Annie on cue and do my jump-up? The doctor shook his head. He said my leg muscles were torn, too. We had spent weeks on those tricks, and now, in a split second under the wheels of a truck, all that work had gone for nothing. But I was lucky not to have been killed, and I knew it.

The next few days passed somehow; I can't remember much about them. I was so groggy that all I can recall is seeing Billy's face from time to time, looking at me sadly and with worry in his eyes. I couldn't even wag my tail to greet him, and I was lying on my side with my legs in a cast, dopey with pain-killers. I couldn't even lift my head, but Billy says that every time I saw him I would put out the tip of my tongue, as if to try to lick his face. It was the only movement I could make.

I was shaky and still in the cast when Bill took me home from the hospital, but I was so thankful to be alive and back again with Billy and my friends that I was happy, even in the cast. And I knew that he'd saved my life, so I wanted to please Bill even more than ever. I wanted to do my tricks for him as soon as I could. So, much, much earlier than anyone had expected, I was back doing them all.

All except one. I have never crawled again. I can't anymore; it's physically impossible. And it's kind of sad, when you think about how hard Billy worked for so long, trying to get me to do that one trick. And how everybody had laughed at him, and cheered when I finally showed I could do it. And I never did do it on stage after all.

But I'm getting ahead of my story. We were almost at opening night. The first performance of *Annie* in a theater. I've heard a lot of actors telling pre-opening stories, but ours will stand up to the best of them.

We have to begin with the dress rehearsal. It was held on a Monday night. First of all, the set was so big that they could barely squeeze it into the theater. It hadn't been used before, it was very complicated scenery, and it didn't work.

As though that weren't enough, that very night, the night of the dress rehearsal, a hurricane came roaring up to Goodspeed and knocked out our lights. Goodspeed had a generator of its own, but it gave very little light, certainly not enough for us to see well. The kids all hated the storm. So we had thunder, lightning, a set that didn't work, six nervous children, and one very sore dog.

We began the rehearsal at nine in the evening. By one-thirty in the morning, we had run through only the first act. At that time, the director called a halt to the rehearsal, and we never did get to run the play all the way through before opening it. What a disaster! Billy and the others marveled that I managed to remain so calm during the long rehearsal and the hurricane. I spent as much of that time as I could asleep on my black vinyl couch. But why shouldn't I be calm? After all the things I had lived through, after my narrow escapes and my brushes with death, why should a little thunder and lightning scare me?

Opening night. Even I was excited, because it was my first night before a real audience, although I'd seen and heard them from the wings many times by now. I was suddenly a working actor, and everything that Billy had taught me was to be put to use at last. I am proud to say that, sore as I was, I performed like what the kids call "a pro."

I came out on stage to applause, and I could feel the affection coming toward me from the audience. People were saying "Ooooh" and "Awwww" and making dog-loving sounds, and it made me so happy I fell in love with audiences right then and there. I still feel that love every time we play, and I try to return it with the best performance I can give. Anyway, even though I was still stiff and hurting that opening night, I came out on cue, lay down on cue, went over to Annie on cue and *jumped up!* The veterinarians had told Bill that I shouldn't, couldn't and wouldn't jump up so soon, but I did. And there was more clapping, and I felt more love coming over the footlights. I even ran off stage on cue, although I'll tell you in a minute about the trouble I ran into later with that trick. But, on opening night, I worked like a dog, if I may say so, and I was a hit.

The show was running three and a half hours, way too long. The reviews, which the kids waited for nervously, all had a kind word to say about me, and Billy was so proud of me that he began to keep a scrapbook of my clippings and reviews.

Then I too ran into some problems. I had become very friendly with the little girl who played Annie. And it upset me and confused me to see those two big "policemen" trying to drag her away, off the stage and back to the orphanage. So, after the first week, when she shouted, "Run, Sandy, run!" at me, I didn't run. Instead, I tried to defend her, staying on the stage. I barked like mad and one night I even tried to bite one of the policemen. They were so real I forgot they were actors, and that night *I* ended up chasing *them* off the stage instead of the other way around.

Of course, I had no idea that I was upsetting what Bill called "the dramatic balance" of the show. The orphan child and the orphan dog were supposed to be separated, but I couldn't part from Annie—it brought back to me so many bad and vivid memories. Billy solved that problem eventually, by having one of the "cops" raise his nightstick and wave it at me. If you'd lived the kind of scary and uncertain life that I had before Billy, you'd be scared at the sight of a stick, too. It chased me right off the stage, every time. Actually, the whole thing proved useful in the end, because later, when my part was enlarged and I *had* to bark at the "cop" on cue, it was easy to learn. I'd already had all that experience.

The second problem was kind of funny. *Annie* was the last show of the 1975 season. Rehearsals were over, the workshop was closed, my training sessions were over, and during the day we would all lie around in the sun and take it easy, just enjoying the summer. I'd already seen two weeks' worth of audiences and taken two weeks' worth of bows, and I was just a little bored. It was lazy time, and I'm afraid I carried it a little far. In the evening I would make my entrance, lie down on cue, and fall fast asleep, right there on stage. When Annie would feed me my cue to come to her, all you could hear in the front rows was my gentle snoring. Or, if I was at least half awake, I'd get up sooooo slowly, and yawn, and stretch, and move over toward Annie like molasses.

I have to admit the audiences ate it up, and it was always good for a laugh, even a round of applause. But it didn't do the pace of the show any good; we were running too long as it was. So Billy had to keep me wide awake. He'd run me around the theater five or six times before curtain, to get my energies up and my juices flowing. Or we'd play a hot game of tug-the-sock, which is still my favorite. Anyway, I'd arrive on stage with my tongue hanging out, but I'd be wide awake.

The last problem I met at Goodspeed wasn't funny; it bewildered me. Two weeks after the show opened, they switched Annies. Andrea McArdle was to be the new Annie. She had been playing the Tough Orphan; now she was coming in as the lead in *two days!*

I had been used to playing on stage with Kristen, and now I was supposed to take my cues from Andrea. Andrea had only forty-eight hours to learn a very long and difficult part; she's on stage for almost the entire show. Only one hour was allotted to her training with me. But Andrea loves dogs, and has a springer spaniel of her own. So she devoted a great deal of her spare time to learning my tricks, and we loved each other right from the beginning. And we still do. She is one of the closest friends I have in the world, and I will love Andrea McArdle while there's a wag left in my tail.

But now the worst thing in the world was happening to me. I had never, never expected it, but I was losing Billy. With two weeks more to run, the show would soon close. But Billy was pulling away from me. I saw him less and less. Other people were spending time with me, on and off the stage. Not Billy. What was happening?

A lot. Billy was scheduled to go back to New York, to begin his classes at New York University again. He lived in a fifth-floor walkup in Greenwich Village, in a house that didn't permit dogs.

His original plan was that, with the publicity that I was getting as an "orphan dog," good homes would be offered to me. And the plan was coming to pass. Not a day went by when I didn't get the offer of a fine home somewhere in Connecticut. Some of those homes included children, others included swimming pools, but none of them included Bill.

I would go to a good home, Bill would go back to school. And that would be that. All Bill had to offer me was five flights of forbidden stairs, a dirty city, and hardly any grass or trees. And himself. But that was all I wanted. Bill Berloni.

So I became very unhappy. I wouldn't do my tricks; I'd just lie there on the stage, missing Billy, wanting Billy. Back in New York, it turned out, Billy was missing me and wanting me. Finally he couldn't take it anymore and he came back to Goodspeed. What a reunion we had! I wagged my whole body with pleasure at seeing him, and he hugged and petted me a lot. When Billy went back to New York, I went with him. *Annie* was over, we thought. How wrong we both were! *Annie* was just beginning.

We drove back to New York at the end of that summer thinking that my stage career was over for good. Apart from my accident, it had been a marvelous summer for both of us, and we were looking forward to settling down to a routine existence in New York, where Billy would be the actor and I would be only his dog.

Five

Before we'd left Goodspeed, there had been some rumors floating around that Mr. Charnin was planning to take *Annie* to Broadway. But all the kids, including Billy, told me not to believe it, that it would never happen. I thought it wouldn't much matter to me one way or another. I had learned to love the theater, to love the lights and the people applauding, to enjoy taking a bow. On the other paw, I love to sleep and just laze around, and be with Billy, so, theater or no, I was happy either way.

But, as it happened, the rumors were true. *Annie* would be produced by the famous Mike Nichols, and would open at the Kennedy Center in Washington, then be brought to New York for a Broadway run. And not only was I supposed to be back in the play, but my part was going to be increased to three times its length, and I would have to learn new tricks for it.

By now, Billy and I were living in New York City, up five flights of stairs in Greenwich Village. The landlord didn't allow dogs, so I had to be extra quiet and careful. Billy and I used to sneak down the stairs twice a day for my exercise, and sneak back up on tiptoe. I couldn't woof or growl, and even my tail-thumping was risky. But we ran around Washington Square Park, and I got plenty of exercise and fresh air. Also, Billy would take me with him to the theater at school. He was majoring in drama at NYU, and he told everybody I had earned the right to be in a theater.

Now we began to concentrate on the new tricks for *Annie*. For the first time, I went to obedience school. Once a week Billy would take me to a professional dog trainer, who would show him how to show me a trick; then Billy would show me. It sometimes confused me. I was now going to have to roll over on cue, and once I'd have to cross the empty stage all by myself, sit down and stare forlornly at the audience, then leave the stage. I was supposed to be looking for Annie. It was my big dramatic moment. The poor lost dog, sniffing the stage for the poor lost girl. It sounds easier than it was to learn.

The only place large enough for us to practice was the street. Billy liked the streets of New York because they had so many people, and automobiles and every kind of traffic, and he thought that if I learned my tricks in the busy streets it would be much easier for me to do them on a busy stage.

But it was fall and getting on to winter when we began, and the streets of New York City are cold, let me tell you. As the winter went on, we were out there every day, practicing and practicing, and my paws and tail began to freeze. There was one part of the trick where I had to sit, and I would lower my tail to one inch above the ground and hold it there. I wasn't about to rest it on the ice-cold sidewalk, and Billy had to be satisfied with that.

Soon a rehearsal hall was chosen uptown, and I began to go to rehearsals. One day, Billy wasn't there; he just left me to rehearse all by myself. When he came to pick me up, he smelled nervous and anxious. I wondered why. When we got home, I found out.

I could smell dog three flights down from our apartment. There was another dog in my house. I must tell you something about myself. I am not fond of other dogs. My past experiences with them, when they chased me away from food and attacked me in my wandering days, left me with a dislike of them. And to sense one in my own home . . . !

Billy opened the door slowly and put himself between me and the doorway, blocking my view. But I peered around his legs and saw him. Another dog. About my size, but very different-looking. A cross between a collie and a golden retriever, I would have guessed. With long, silky fur and stand-up ears. Another dog in my home. I began to growl, low in my throat.

"Sandy," Billy said nervously. "This is Arf. This is your understudy."

Why did I need an understudy? I have never missed a performance in my life. We'll see about this, I thought, and I ducked around Billy's legs and started for this "Arf" or whatever his name was. I would make short work of this intruder, and send him yelping down five flights of stairs.

But Arf was cringing, abject, his dark eyes pleading with me. Why, he was only a puppy, really! Suddenly, a rush of unwanted, unhappy memories poured over me, and I remembered my own cringing days, and the love that Billy and others had shown me, a love that had kept me safe and warm. I wasn't eager to share that love, but love doesn't get cut in half when you share it; it doubles.

So I stopped in midbound and walked forward slowly instead. I sniffed the pup all over, checking him out. He was okay. I sniffed him again, and he sniffed me back. I poked at him with my paw,

54

and he poked me back. Suddenly we were playing, racing around the small apartment together. And we've been playing ever since.

Arf learned all my tricks, and I worked in the rehearsal hall with Andrea McArdle, who was going to be *Annie* again. We renewed our old friendship, and rehearsed like the buddies we are. Everyone talks about what a fine actress and a magnificent singer she is, but to me she is, mostly, a friend. Now we were going to be in the big time together.

Things were very different now for the *Annie* crowd. This was Broadway, and nothing but the best for us. Theoni V. Aldredge, the famous designer, did the costumes for the show, and even I got one. She designed a special large red bow for me, to wear in the final, Christmas scene, and it was made especially to my measure: I wear a size eleven.

Then, almost before I knew it, the New York rehearsal time was over, and we were all going to Washington, where *Annie* was to open at the Eisenhower Theatre in the John F. Kennedy Center for the Performing Arts. Winter was nearly over; we went down to Washington in the last week of February. Billy, Arf and I were given a terrific place to stay, in Alexandria, right near a large fenced-in playground that had room enough for Arf and me to run around in.

As for the theater, it's in a large building, all of white Italian marble, and it's decorated with many valuable gifts and works of art donated by other nations. Billy took me to look at all of them. The theater itself is very beautiful; it seats 1,300 people and it has red carpets everywhere, and crystal chandeliers that dazzled my eyes whenever I happened to look up.

But the greenroom was my favorite hangout. It was as different from Goodspeed as prime ribs are from canned dog food. It was a luxurious place, and the first thing I made a beeline for was, of

course, the couch. The couch at Goodspeed had been an old black vinyl thing. This one was new green satin. But to me, a couch is a couch, someplace for me to rest my weary bones between the acts. So, naturally, I grabbed it. The greenroom became my dressing room for the Washington run, and the couch my own personal property. As for Arf, well, he wasn't always mindful of his manners, so he wasn't allowed on any of the furniture. He wasn't even allowed on the carpet. He spent the entire Washington run on a large piece of plastic spread on the floor of the greenroom.

Just as I was settling in at Washington, an unsettling thing happened. Billy just wasn't there much anymore. He was away most of the time. I was used to spending almost every hour of the night and day with him. I needed him and I thought he needed me. But maybe he didn't, after all. I tried to fight the loneliness, but it kept coming back. On our first preview night, the audience loved me and cheered me, but I knew that I had cheated them. I hadn't done all my tricks the best way I knew how. I had rehearsed them until I had them perfect down to the last tail-wag, but my heart just wasn't in it. I was okay, but not perfect. Because I was missing Billy so much.

It wasn't until later that I learned what Bill had been going through and why he was absent so much. Bill's life had been tied up with mine so much that he was neglecting his own. In order to stay with me in Washington, he'd have to drop out of all his classes, give up his education, and lose all the money he'd paid for his NYU tuition. He thought that by pulling away from me now he could get me used to working with somebody else in the wings by the time *Annie* opened in New York. But all this was hurting him as much as it was hurting me. It had happened before, at Goodspeed, when Billy went back to New York without me. I just

57

My understudy, Arf, is *always* in the background.

couldn't do good work without Bill. I didn't want to. Love was the bond between us, and I would do anything for that special love.

But just as things were looking blackest for Billy and me, we received help in the form of Mrs. Roger Stevens, wife of the head of the Kennedy Center. Mrs. Stevens heads up the Animal Welfare League and is one of the most dedicated workers in Washington for animal legislation. She became a friend to Billy and me when we were needing one most. She arranged for Bill to have a place to stay and to earn some money. And she understood that Billy and I could not be happy apart; she helped him to decide that his education could wait but that I could not.

So Bill dropped out of school, to work with me in the show, and I was happy again. Once again, I did all my tricks well.

By the third night of previews, it was plain that *Annie* was a very big hit. I could never see an empty seat in the theater, and the clapping was much louder than at Goodspeed because there were so many more people.

With Bill and me together again, and *Annie* a hit, what more did we need to make us happy? We got it. On March 4, we went to the White House, at the invitation of the President of the United States.

"It's the White House, Sandy," Billy said to me as we came past the uniformed guards and Secret Service men. "The President and Mrs. Carter live there. It's the most important place in the world."

Just to show I understood, I left a little of myself behind, just beyond the shrubbery.

President Carter was entertaining the governors of the fifty states; it was the first time he had met with all of them together. As entertainment for them and their spouses, the President and

Mrs. Carter had requested a special short production of *Annie*. We were going to do highlights from the show. A platform, not quite a stage, had been erected for us in the East Room.

The East Room of the White House was the best place I'd seen yet, better even than the greenroom of the theater. There were fancy blue brocade sofas, and, naturally, I headed for one immediately, but Billy kept a tight hand on my leash. Why not? I thought—a sofa is a sofa. The room was too large and dazzling for me to take in all at once, but I could make out large crystal chandeliers, tall windows covered in gold brocade, a large fireplace, and a very grand piano, not like any I'd seen in the rehearsal hall or the theater. This one was huge, and it had gold eagles for legs. Later, Bill told me that President Franklin D. Roosevelt himself had designed that piano, and that the body of John F. Kennedy had lain in state in the East Room before it was moved to the Capitol Rotunda.

If I may say so, the performance went off very well. I had three costume changes: the old piece of rope I wear in the early part of the show, the red Theoni V. Aldredge ribbon I wear in the last scene, and a black tie to change into for the reception afterward, to which all of us had been invited.

The President and Mrs. Carter greeted us. Amy wasn't there, because it was a school night, but she did come to a matinee a day or so later, and she brought some of her schoolmates. After the show, she brought them backstage and came right in to see me. Amy Carter threw her arms around my neck and gave me a big hug. Boy, was that a thrill! As good as any movie star.

The governors all wanted to meet the stars. The governor of Connecticut is Ella T. Grasso, and she had seen *Annie* twice at Goodspeed. So she not only knew me, she was proud of me.

"This dog is from *my* state," Mrs. Grasso told the other governors, and she gave my ears a nice rub. "He's from one of our Humane Societies." She kept calling all the other governors over to meet me, and soon my paw became tired from all that shaking. But I ate up the attention, I have to confess. I never get tired of being loved.

After our evening at the White House, *Annie* previewed for

four days and then opened officially. I could tell from Billy's grin that we got rave reviews. The word came from New York that people were already lining up there to buy tickets. Excitement was flowing through all of us as we ended our Washington run. It had been a wonderful experience; we had been a big hit and had been treated like royalty. Now Broadway lay ahead of us, and Broadway was "it." The home of the theater, the really Big Time.

Six

*T*hey say that if you haven't made it in New York, you haven't made it. We all knew that New York was waiting for us, but we weren't sure just what reception they'd give us. Opening night at the Alvin was an experience for me, even though I'd already been through two openings, Goodspeed and the Eisenhower Theatre. But New York is different.

Dogs sense everything, you know. We can tell a human's mood by a kind of magical perception, especially when we love a human as I love Billy. He was so excited, and so was Andrea, that even I, who am usually fairly calm, became excited and ran around barking before the curtain went up. There was a kind of stirring in the audience, a kind of expectation that all the actors felt. And I felt it, too, and it put me on my mettle. I guess you'd say I had a case of opening-night jitters.

Things were very different for me now. For one thing, I had my own dressing room, on a floor all to myself. I was gracious enough to share it with Arf, but the dressing room was mine, not ours. In the mirror over the dressing table, where actors always stick their good-luck telegrams, were a bunch of opening-night telegrams for me, telling me to sprain a paw. ("Break a leg" is how we theater people wish one another good luck.) Around the mirror were lights, just like on any star's dressing mirror. And in my

Every star has his own personal dresser.

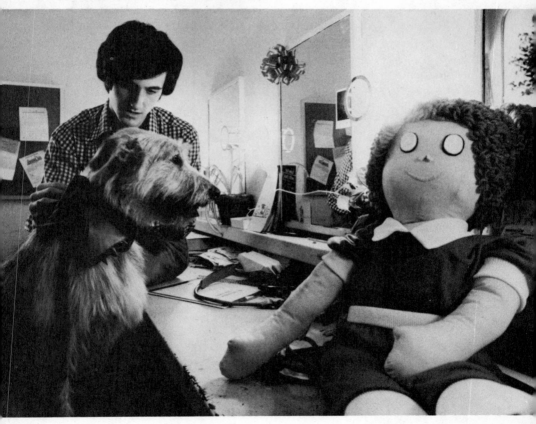

Some of the scenes Andrea
McArdle and I steal in *Annie* . . .

. . . but even Arf has a moment of glory!

room were gifts of flowers, chew toys, rubber bones—although Billy's sock will always be my favorite toy. My publicity had preceded me to Broadway, and I was making new friends all the time.

I don't think we were worried about the audience; everybody loved *Annie* anywhere we went. But we had heard that the New York stage critics are a hardened bunch. They have seen everything, and they are very hard to please. *Annie* is a show filled with old-fashioned sentiment and optimism. New York is a town that they say has no heart. How would New York take to *Annie?*

Well, New York loved us; even the tough critics laughed and cried and cheered. Who says New York has no heart? For *Annie,* it was all heart. They loved everybody—Andrea, and Reid Shelton, Dorothy Loudon and even me. In fact, a lot of them loved especially me.

Everybody in the theater knows what it's like to wait, heart in mouth, for the first reviews to appear. But now that television news covers the theater, you usually don't have to wait for the morning papers to find out how well or badly you scored. Our first review was on the CBS late news. Pat Collins told her audience that *Annie* deserved to run for fifty years, and she mentioned me, Sandy, as a "mongrel dog" who was "the co-star." Me, a co-star!

Instantly, *Annie* became a smash. There wasn't an empty seat in the theater. It became the hottest ticket, the hardest to come by, on all of Broadway. And every night, when I made my entrance slinking out on the stage, I heard cheers from the audience. And I could hear the little kids yelling, "Look! There's Sandy! It's Sandy!"

That's one of the things I enjoy most about *Annie.* There are so many kids present at every performance. You can always tell where they're sitting, because of their laughter. I love children's

So *many* requests!

laughter, and I love the way they wait for me after the show, wanting my picture or my pawdograph.

After the opening, *Annie* got a lot of publicity, and some of it was about me. The columnist Earl Wilson, who is a dog lover, was very good to me and wrote about me often, and ran my picture in his column. Feature writers came to me and Billy, because they were interested in the story of a dog who was doomed to die but became a star instead. Andrea and I made the cover of *Cue* magazine, and we posed for other magazines too. I even got used to flashbulbs, although I can't honestly say I like them.

A big change that happened because of *Annie*'s success was that Billy, Arf and I moved into a larger apartment, right near Central Park. No more five-story walkups for us. The landlord even knows that Arf and I live there. Our new apartment is com-

Three heroic dogs—Sandy, Balto and Arf

I am a meat-and-potatoes dog,
and Gallagher's has the best. . . .

All of us theater folk go to Sardi's.

But I like dessert too, at Rumpelmayer's.

fortable and roomy, and we have the park next door, so we get plenty of fresh air and exercise. Sometimes I'm recognized on the street and in the park, and people have been really nice to us.

Our social life included going to the Tony Awards; both of us dressed in black tie, to watch *Annie* win seven awards, including "best musical." I wish there had been an animal category, but Billy said that would be very unusual.

Things began to get hectic for us. The Sunday *New York Times Magazine* sent Anna Quindlen down to interview Billy and me; Richard Avedon photographed me for *Vogue; New York* magazine put me on one of its covers, along with Ambassador Andrew Young, jockey Steve Cauthen and other celebrities. The details of my new life began to be in the public domain: how I eat ice cream at Rumpelmayer's; how I met Paul McCartney; how I put my head on Liv Ullmann's lap; how much money I make; how I go back and forth to the Alvin Theater in a Checker cab; how Gallagher's restaurant sends me steak and roast-beef bones.

But other things stand out in my mind as highlights. I was chosen official mascot for the Floating Hospital, which is a large ship that takes more than forty thousand kids, eight hundred at a time, on a cruise that is combined with diagnosis and treatment, so that the kids have a good time and learn more about good health. Later in the summer, when the Floating Hospital accepted its five millionth child, I was asked back a second time. It was a big party, and Mayor Beame was there. There was a giant cake, and when they cut it they gave me the first bite. It all made me very proud. Me, just a pound hound.

I was less proud when the kids from the *Bad News Bears* movies licked the kids from *Annie* in exhibition baseball. (I was mascot again, and I wore a T-shirt with my name on it, and a baseball cap,

but Arf ate the elastic off the cap, and it kept falling down over my eyes and sliding off my ears.) But what chance did we have against professional ball players who had made baseball their game through two movies?

And, of course, I was asked to write my life story, which I have enjoyed doing. The bad parts were tough for me to relive, but if telling the story of my life should save the lives of other dogs and cats, then it was all worth it. If people stop breeding their animals and start adopting them from shelters, there won't be any more hard-luck stories like mine. Mine ends happily, but thousands of other animals suffer agonizing slow starvation, disease and injury when they're abandoned. If I have any message for the world, it's this: Neuter your pets, and adopt new ones. Don't ever take an animal you won't be taking for keeps.

I guess I must be one of the luckiest dogs in the world. I'm sure that I'm the happiest. I love being in the show; I love our new home; I love Billy and I guess I even love Arf.

Home is the best place there is. I never have to do my tricks there, I can just lie around and snooze. At night, Arf and I both sleep on Billy's bed, sometimes in it. He says he feels like the peanut butter in a sandwich, but he never throws us out.

I'm me, and Billy respects that. Sometimes I don't do all my tricks on stage, and there are hollers from the brass, and memos. And Billy says, "He's a dog. Remember? Dogs don't read memos. Let him be himself. They love him no matter what." Sometimes, when Billy wants me to do something, I just cock my head to one side and sit there looking at him. He gets so frustrated; it's enough to make a cat laugh. He knows that I know what he wants, and I know he knows. And I know that he'll never raise his hand to punish me, and he knows that I know. It's like a circle, with me in the middle, teasing. But I always give in.

I love going to the theater to work. I lie at home half snoozing until Billy starts getting dressed. When I see his shirt and jeans go on, I stand up, yawn and stretch. Excitement begins to build up

inside me as he puts on his shoes. The minute the second shoe is on, I start jumping up and down, and by the time Bill says, "Do you want to go to the theater, Sandy?" I'm already at the door, pawing at the knob. I like riding there in those big Checker cabs, too. I never had anything like that in my earlier life.

In the theater they call, "Thirty minutes," then "Fifteen minutes," then "Places, please." At five minutes, Billy and Andrea and I meet on the stage and play together to get warmed up, and nobody ever bothers us. It's one of the best times of the day, when I am with the two people I love most in the world. Billy says that the theater must be in my blood, that I'm a real ham. One night I wouldn't get off the stage, because I was enjoying the applause so much; I just sat there and wagged my tail for more. And got it.

I use up a lot of energy in the theater. When the show is over, I'm ready for my dinner and some sleep. Arf is sometimes a thorn in my side, although I hate to say it. He loves being awake, and he loves to play. Just as I'm settling down for a fine snooze, he'll wake me up by dropping the sock on my face. He knows that's all it takes to get a game going. I have received a lot of presents, and our house is filled with rubber and nylon toys. Arf plays with them all, especially with a hard rubber ball that he's slowly demolishing with his teeth. My only toy, the only one I cherish, is a raggedy sock of Billy's, with knots tied in it for chewing. I've had it since Goodspeed; it's *mine*. Naturally, Arf is after it all the time, and he uses it as blackmail to get me into a game when I want to sleep. As soon as I see that sock—*my* sock—in Arf's jaws, I'm up and after it. We rough-and-tumble and drag it around until Arf is worn out, too, then we curl up together and sleep. At night, we push our way into Billy's room and ignore his protests. It's a good life.

My future doesn't worry me. Nothing worries me. I have Billy to look after me, and he makes the decisions. So far, they've all been good ones; I'm sure the ones to come will be just as good. Life takes many paths, and it doesn't pay to worry in advance about how many rocks there are in each road. Especially if you can use the time to sleep. We've been poor together, Billy and I, and it was

okay. Now we're doing better, and it's still okay. The time may come when I won't be working, and that will be okay, too. As long as Billy is there. He's not my owner; we're more like brothers. Oh, and Arf too. He can come along.

One thing I know. The really bad times are over for good. Love and patience rescued me and brought me a new life. I have finished with looking back. Now I only want to look ahead, to even better times to come. And, whatever Sandy does in the future, whatever Billy does in the future, we'll do it together, a dog and his boy.